T0394897

THE HISTORY OF FOODS
CANDY

by Kristine Spanier, MLIS

pogo

Ideas for Parents and Teachers

Pogo Books let children practice reading informational text while introducing them to nonfiction features such as headings, labels, sidebars, maps, and diagrams, as well as a table of contents, glossary, and index.

Carefully leveled text with a strong photo match offers early fluent readers the support they need to succeed.

Before Reading

- "Walk" through the book and point out the various nonfiction features. Ask the student what purpose each feature serves.
- Look at the glossary together. Read and discuss the words.

During Reading

- Have the child read the book independently.
- Invite them to list questions that arise from reading.

After Reading

- Discuss the child's questions. Talk about how they might find answers to those questions.
- Prompt the child to think more. Ask: What is your favorite candy? Do you know when and how it was invented?

Pogo Books are published by Jump!
3500 American Blvd W, Suite 150
Bloomington, MN 55431
www.jumplibrary.com

Copyright © 2026 Jump!
International copyright reserved in all countries.
No part of this book may be reproduced in any form without written permission from the publisher.

Jump! is a division of FlutterBee Education Group.

Library of Congress Cataloging-in-Publication Data

Names: Spanier, Kristine, author.
Title: Candy / by Kristine Spanier, MLIS.
Description: Minneapolis, MN: Jump!, Inc., [2026]
Series: The history of foods | Includes index.
Audience: Ages 7–10
Identifiers: LCCN 2024054518 (print)
LCCN 2024054519 (ebook)
ISBN 9798892139007 (hardcover)
ISBN 9798892139014 (paperback)
ISBN 9798892139021 (ebook)
Subjects: LCSH: Candy—History—Juvenile literature.
Inventors—History—Juvenile literature.
Classification: LCC TX792 .S63 2026 (print)
LCC TX792 (ebook)
DDC 641.85/309—dc23/eng/20241205
LC record available at https://lccn.loc.gov/2024054518
LC ebook record available at https://lccn.loc.gov/2024054519

Editor: Jenna Gleisner
Designer: Molly Ballanger

Photo Credits: Holiday.Photo.Top/Shutterstock, cover; Charles Brutlag/Shutterstock, 1; Philip Kinsey/Shutterstock, 3; Andrew Sutherland/Dreamstime, 4; Jmcanally/Shutterstock, 5; Csavvj/Wikimedia, 6-7 (foreground); Pixel-Shot/Shutterstock, 6-7 (background); Courtesy of Hershey Community Archives, Hershey, PA, 8 (left), 9 (foreground), 10-11; Maria Tebriaeva/Shutterstock, 8 (top right); MaraZe/Shutterstock, 8 (bottom right); Julia Metkalova/Shutterstock, 9 (background); Courtesy of Made In Chicago Museum, 12-13 (left); Steven Cukrov/Dreamstime, 12-13 (right); sav_an_dreas/Shutterstock, 14-15; Keith Homan/Shutterstock, 15, 16-17tl (foreground); Aninka Bongers-Sutherland/Shutterstock, 16-17tl (background); bestv/Shutterstock, 16-17tr (foreground), 21 (Skittles); Laura Fokkema/Shutterstock, 16-17tr (background); ZikG/Shutterstock, 16-17bl (foreground); Sophia Cole/Shutterstock, 16-17bl (background); Veronica Winters/Shutterstock, 16-17br; The Image Party/Shutterstock, 18; Sheila Fitzgerald/Shutterstock, 19; Tada Images/Shutterstock, 20-21; Shutterstock, 21; Dreamstime, 21; P Maxwell Photography/Shutterstock, 23.

Printed in the United States of America at Corporate Graphics in North Mankato, Minnesota.

TABLE OF CONTENTS

CHAPTER 1
First Sweet Treats................................4

CHAPTER 2
Candy Bars and More.......................8

CHAPTER 3
Selling Candy....................................18

QUICK FACTS & TOOLS
Timeline..22
Glossary...23
Index..24
To Learn More................................24

CHAPTER 1

FIRST SWEET TREATS

Do you know what the first candy sold in the United States was? It was Gibralters! They were hard, white candies. The **flavors** were lemon and peppermint. Mary Spencer **invented** them. She sold them from pails in Salem, Massachusetts. In 1806, she opened America's first candy store!

Pharmacists helped make candy popular. They added sugar to **lozenges** to mask the taste of medicine. People ate them like candy! In 1847, Oliver Chase made candy wafers without any medicine. He used a **press**. They became Necco wafers!

CHAPTER 1

CHAPTER 1

In 1869, Gustav Goelitz started a candy business. It made butter creams like candy corn. At first, candy corn was called Chicken Feed. Boxes had a rooster on them. The candy's **slogan** was, "Something worth crowing for."

CHAPTER 2

CANDY BARS AND MORE

Milton Hershey wanted to make candy. He **experimented** with caramel. It had been made with wax. But it stuck to people's teeth. Hershey learned that fresh milk made better caramel.

Milton Hershey

Next, Hershey wanted to make chocolate. He had tried Swiss chocolate. It was milky and sweet. He spent seven years trying to copy the **recipe**. He sold the first Hershey's Milk Chocolate Bar in 1900. It was just five cents!

10 CHAPTER 2

Hershey finished building his chocolate **factory** in 1905. In 1907, Hershey's Kisses were introduced.

For 14 years, each Hershey's Kiss was wrapped by hand. In 1921, the first foil-wrapping machine was created.

DID YOU KNOW?

Hershey gave a lot of his own money to build the town of Hershey, Pennsylvania. Streetlights in the town look like Hershey's Kisses!

CHAPTER 2

Frank Mars started his first candy business in 1920. In 1923, he and his son created a chocolate bar. It was filled with nougat and caramel. It was the Milky Way! In 1930, he created a new recipe. He added peanuts. It was the Snickers Bar.

The **Great Depression** started in 1929. People did not have much money for treats. Candymakers created penny candy. Tootsie Rolls, taffy, and candy buttons were some. They cost just one cent!

WHAT DO YOU THINK?

The Snickers Bar was named after a horse. What would you name a candy bar? Why?

1940s

2020s

CHAPTER 2

14 CHAPTER 2

In the 1960s, the Goelitz company started making jelly beans. Today, it is the Jelly Belly Candy Company. It makes more than 100 flavors of jelly beans.

DID YOU KNOW?

Do you know the most popular Jelly Belly flavor? It is Very Cherry!

Pop Rocks were first sold in 1975. They pop and fizz on your tongue. Next came Skittles. Then came Nerds in 1983. Warheads were first sold in the United States in 1993. They are sour!

WHAT DO YOU THINK?

Each American eats about 22 pounds (10 kilograms) of candy a year. Do you think this is a little or a lot? How much do you think you eat?

CHAPTER 2

TASTE
THE
EXPLOSION

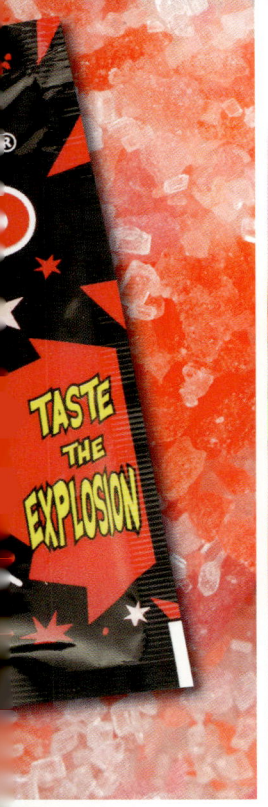

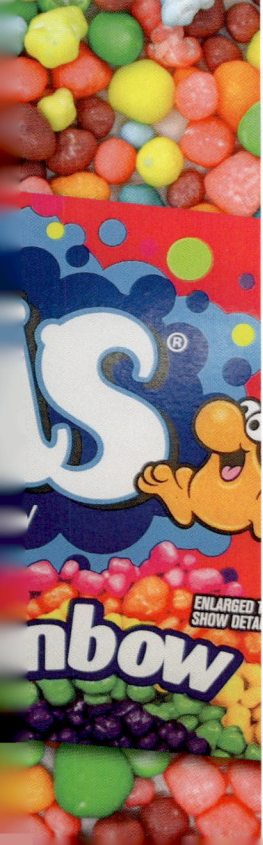

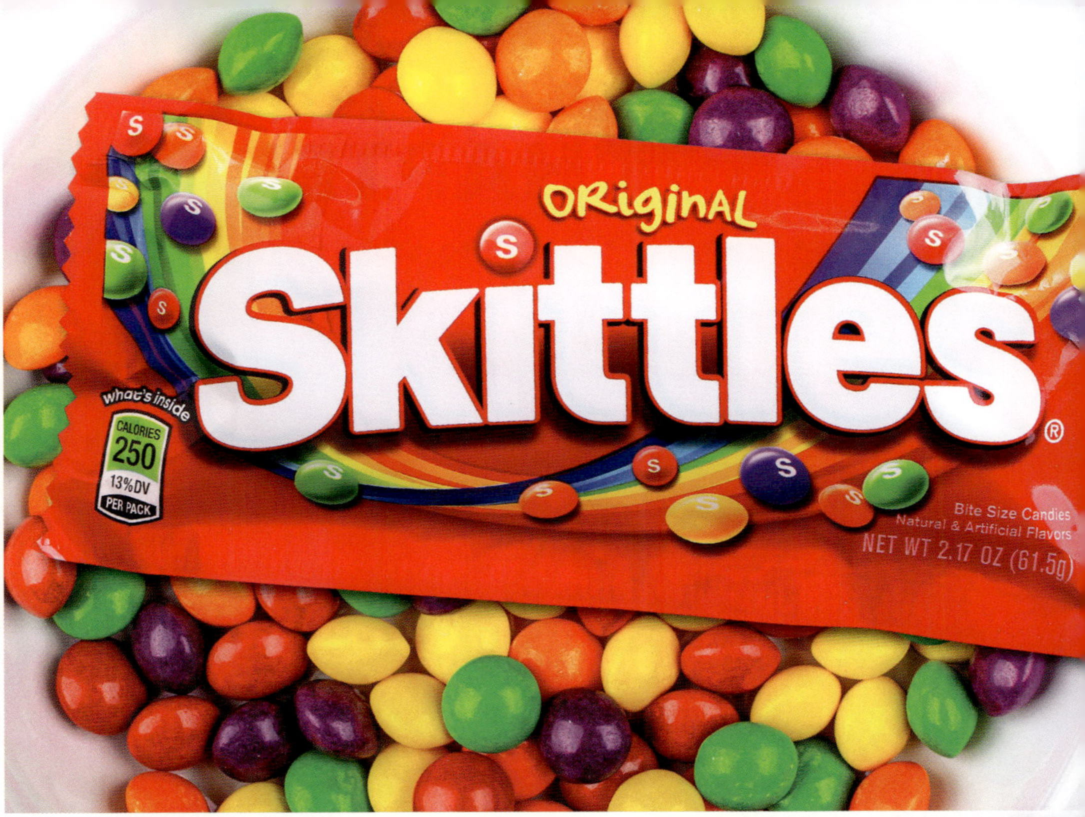
ORiginAL
Skittles
what's inside
CALORIES
250
13%DV
PER PACK
Bite Size Candies
Natural & Artificial Flavors
NET WT 2.17 OZ (61.5g)

nbow

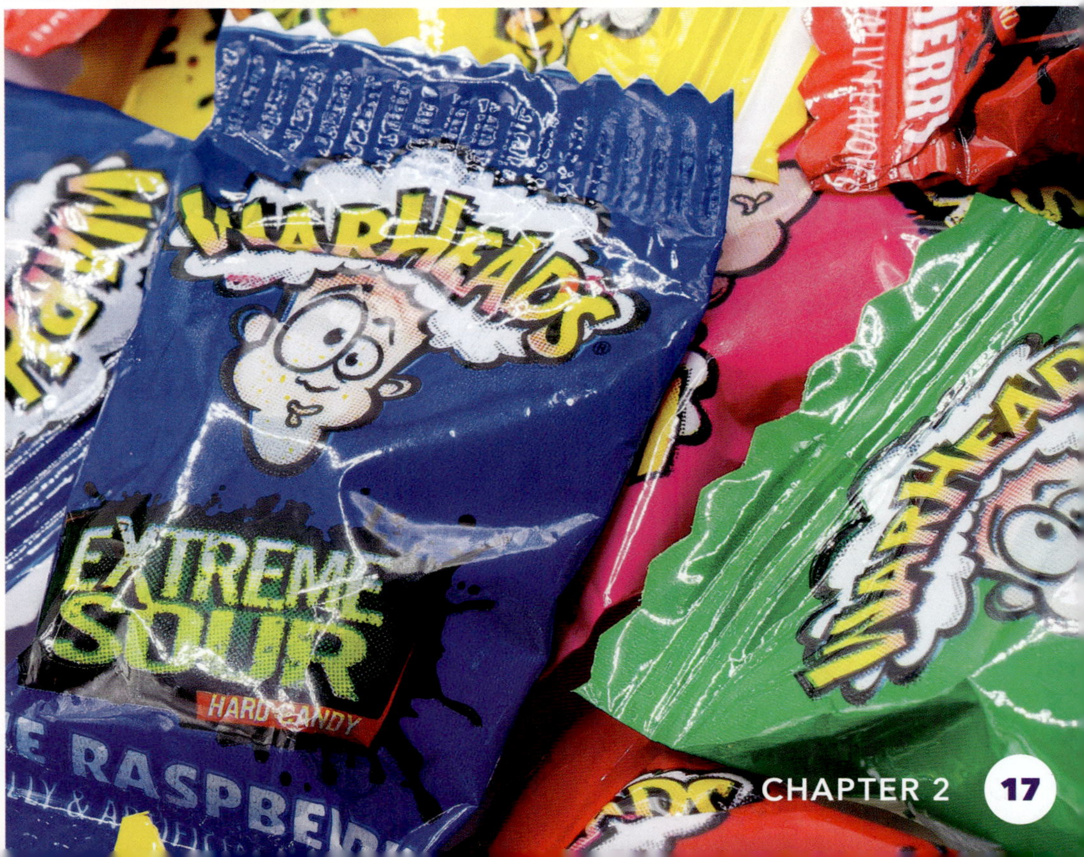
WARHEADS
EXTREME
SOUR
HARD CANDY
WARHEADS

CHAPTER 3

SELLING CANDY

Candy is popular for its taste. Companies **market** it, too. One way is to give it a catchy name like Whatchamacallit. Another way is to place it in checkout lines at the store. Why? People see it and want to buy it.

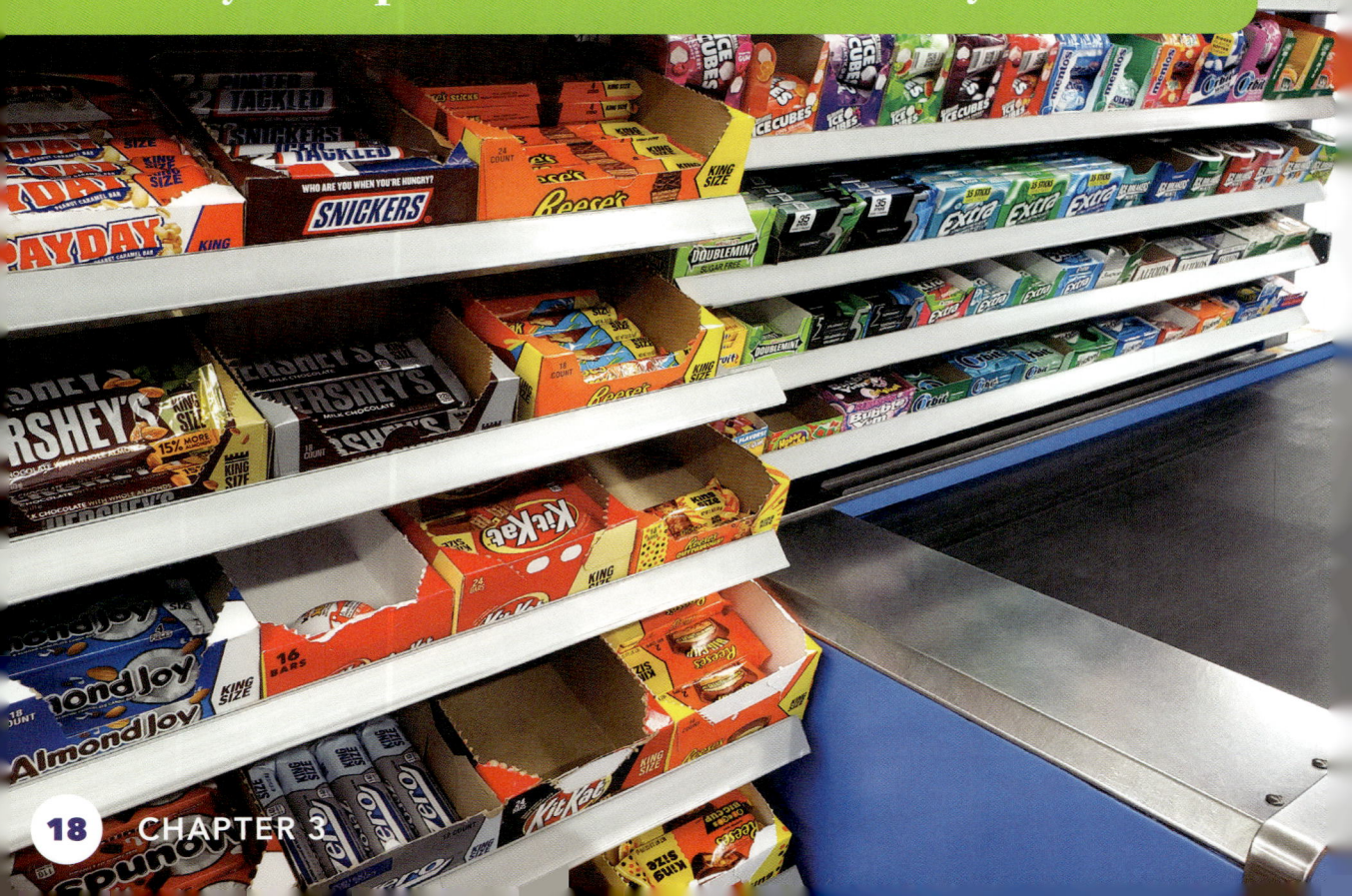

Advertisements tie candy to holidays. They tell us candy should be part of the fun. People buy even more!

CHAPTER 3 19

Candy wrappers often have bright colors. They catch our attention. Candy is sweet and fun! What is your favorite kind?

TAKE A LOOK!

Candy wrappers come in many colors. Take a look!

CHAPTER 3 · 21

QUICK FACTS & TOOLS

Take a look at some important dates in the history of candy!

1806
The first U.S. candy store opens.

2023
Chocolate and candy sales in the United States reach an all-time high of $48 billion.

1847
Oliver Chase invents Necco wafers.

1960s
The Goelitz company starts making jelly beans.

1900
Hershey sells the first Milk Chocolate Bar.

1975
Pop Rocks are sold for the first time.

1923
Frank Mars and his son invent the Milky Way candy bar.

GLOSSARY

advertisements: Commercials, posters, or other methods that show or tell about a product or service so people want to buy or use it.

experimented: Tested or tried something in order to learn something particular.

factory: A building in which products are made in large numbers, often using machines.

flavors: Tastes.

Great Depression: A period of severe economic decline. The Great Depression began in 1929 and lasted through the 1930s.

invented: Created and produced for the first time.

lozenges: Small, flavored medicines designed to be held in the mouth and slowly dissolve.

market: To share information about a product to convince people to buy it.

pharmacists: People who are trained to prepare and give out medicines.

press: A machine that uses pressure to shape, flatten, squeeze, or stamp.

recipe: Instructions for preparing food, including what ingredients are needed.

slogan: A word or phrase used to attract attention.

INDEX

candy corn 7

candy store 4

Chase, Oliver 5

flavors 4, 15

Gibralters 4

Goelitz, Gustav 7

Great Depression 12

Hershey, Milton 8, 9, 11

Hershey's Kisses 11

Hershey's Milk Chocolate Bar 9

Jelly Belly Candy Company 15

Mars, Frank 12

Milky Way 12

Necco wafers 5

Nerds 16

Pop Rocks 16

recipe 9, 12

Skittles 16

Snickers Bar 12

Spencer, Mary 4

taffy 12

Tootsie Rolls 12

Warheads 16

wrappers 11, 20, 21

TO LEARN MORE

Finding more information is as easy as 1, 2, 3.

❶ Go to www.factsurfer.com

❷ Enter "candy" into the search box.

❸ Choose your book to see a list of websites.